# All Born Perfect

# All Born Perfect

Poems by

Carla Drysdale

Kelsay Books

© 2019 Carla Drysdale. All rights reserved.
This material may not be reproduced in any form, published,
reprinted, recorded, performed, broadcast,
rewritten or redistributed without
the explicit permission of Carla Drysdale.
All such actions are strictly prohibited by law.

Cover design: Shay Culligan

ISBN: 978-1-950462-19-3

Kelsay Books Inc.

kelsaybooks.com

502 S 1040 E, A119
American Fork, Utah 84003

For Jonathan, David and Rafael

# Acknowledgments

I wish to thank Finishing Line Press for publishing my chapbook of poems, *Inheritance*, in 2016, which includes the following poems in this book: *All Born Perfect, The Braid, Chore, Clemency on the Q Train, Dwarf Beech in July, First Night in Rougemont, The Gaze, Giving Up on Revenge, Hunkered, Ice Storm in Port Stanley, Insomnia, Labyrinth, Leap, Miscarriage, Newborn's Mouth, The Next Life, Motherhood Invents Me, Rafael's Question, Recognition, Sonogram* and *Workday*.

*Chore* was published as a numbered broadside by Paris Press for the Associated Writers Program (AWP) conference in 2017.

*Elegy for Leonard Cohen, Earn My Keep* and *Frontalier* were published in 2017 by *What Rough Beast,* a project of Indolent Books.

*Evensong, Labyrinth* and *The Bright Hem* were published by *Tower Journal* in 2016.

*5 a.m.* was published by *Cleaver Magazine* in 2015 and then sent to email subscribers of *Every Day Poems T.S. Poetry Press* in June 2018.

In 2014 *Inheritance* was awarded *PRISM international's* annual Earle Birney Poetry Prize.

My gratitude for writing support and friendship goes to Michelle Bailat-Jones, Michael Broder, Elizabeth Coleman, Sharon Guskin, Kasey Jueds, Jen Kirwin, Cindy Frenkel, Camala Projansky and Julia Shipley. I am grateful for the online nurturing of the Binder of Women Poets. Thank you to my poetry mentor Molly Peacock, for always being there.

Deep gratitude goes to Karen Kelsay and the staff of Kelsay Books for making the poems of *All Born Perfect* become a book.

Many of these poems were written and revised during fellowships at the Virginia Center for the Creative Arts as well as during stays at the Abbaye de la Fille-Dieu in Romont, Switzerland.

Thanks also to my family as well as past, present and future friends.

# Contents

## I

| | |
|---|---|
| The Door Opens to All | 17 |
| Inheritance | 18 |
| Chore | 19 |
| Hunkered | 20 |
| Near Sparta, Ontario | 22 |
| Learning a New Word is a Different Kind of Birth | 23 |
| Labyrinth | 24 |
| Jogging Bra | 25 |
| Insomnia | 27 |
| Ice Storm in Port Stanley | 28 |
| Giving Up on Revenge | 29 |
| Dwarf Beech in July | 30 |
| Scar | 31 |
| Ombres Chinoises | 32 |
| The Gaze | 34 |

## II

| | |
|---|---|
| Taking Things Apart to Live | 37 |
| Miscarriage | 38 |
| Sonogram | 39 |
| Subway tunnel | 40 |
| The Braid | 41 |
| Newborn's Mouth | 42 |
| Recognition | 43 |
| Workday | 44 |
| Earn My Keep | 45 |
| Leap | 46 |
| Rondeau After Meeting Her New Baby | 47 |

| | |
|---|---|
| Clemency on the Q Train | 48 |
| Breadwinner | 49 |
| Layoff | 50 |
| Motherhood Invents Me | 51 |

## III

| | |
|---|---|
| Rafael's Question | 55 |
| Frontalier | 56 |
| First night in Rougemont | 57 |
| The Next Life | 58 |
| Gill, Massachusetts | 59 |
| Large Subject; Small Poem | 60 |
| Hammurabi Replica at the International Labour Office | 61 |
| Blue Poles | 62 |
| Sky Eyes | 63 |
| Elegy for Leonard Cohen | 64 |
| Writing at the Convent of St. Helena | 65 |
| Opened Up | 66 |
| Sanctuary | 67 |
| The Bright Hem | 68 |
| Evensong | 69 |
| All Born Perfect | 71 |
| 5 a.m. | 73 |
| I've Heard the Mermaids | 74 |

I

# The Door Opens to All

We're first for takeoff. A door shut
then speed and voluminous, voluptuous
lifting of wing and wheel.

Clouds cast shadows
over fields, rivers, houses
where people live.

Then the clouds themselves take over,
blocking out the view and I see
only white banks, a blank page.

I used to write your praises, Lord,
for pages and pages at a time.
Then one by one I gave away

or left behind my Bibles: beloved
leather-bound with passages highlighted,
the King James version, the Good News,

the Concordance with Greek and Hebrew
roots explained in English.
Wherever they are

they're gone from me now.
For a few more minutes
I'm on the inside, squinting out

before the plane descends
and the door opens to all that is there.

# Inheritance

One of my two sons devours books
as I did, bespectacled, silent.

There are childhood facts I'd like to check,
but the past is unpopular

with my mother. Her husband wasn't a reader.
His eye was on me during the day

and at night, when the door opened
and carved a wedge of hall light

into my dark room. I would wait for it.
Her pain was mine when

I heard the hush through the wall
after one of their bedroom fights

and her fall into Valium numbness.
My other son peers into

the legacy behind my eyes,
at what I'm trying to hide.

His pleasure and pain
are always mine

as when he kisses his cat or bends
his pen in half and yells at me,

enraged by the words
on the page
in front of him.

# Chore

My mother
waits again for
me to get
in the car
leave it all
God is good
I've forgotten
again
telling things
smelling the rich
honky-tonk song
she wore
to cover herself
pitching horse shit

Never understood
why I had to write
the truth
go to church
to God
to stay alive
to come home
drunk on words, wine
I've written about
animal scent
mother's purple suede coat
like a mantle
all those pre-dawn mornings
in the barn

# Hunkered

My father brings in sagging boxes
softened by years
stacked in storage, waiting for me.

Now they hunker on the living
room floor of his bachelor
apartment this hot day.

My sons and their dad escape
to a translucent pool while I rip open
box after box.

I find books mostly, with advice
on becoming a writer, plus diaries, cards,
articles I'd written for trade magazines,

a few college essays, high school
year-books. Love letters to and from
people I'd be uncomfortable

around now. My hair is heavy, curling
with humidity as I lean into the late
afternoon dust.

Words slide through my
grimy hands. Thankful my fingertips
are blind, I salvage only enough

for a carry-on. My father tries
to recapture lost time, talking to me
about his life and loneliness

the color of faded lottery tickets.
I can't remember my mother and him
ever being together.

My kids and husband reappear, smelling
of coconut sunscreen and chlorine. They pick
through things: a cedar box with a key,

my amateur still life drawings
which they insist we keep. My father
will deal with what we leave behind.

# Near Sparta, Ontario

There was a time I lay
In long field grass,
On a hill near woods
Letting sun burn my freckled skin.

*Blue tin sky*
*Sharp smell of hay*
*My own true spot*

In four summers of growing
I didn't know my childhood
Would end when my mother left.

To the hidden Hermit Thrush
Twitching its head
I seemed unafraid despite the signs—

Her new-found love,
Her husband stalking her
Our boxer dog cowering
Before the beatings.

# Learning a New Word is a Different Kind of Birth

The divine cut out of her when her mother

died, turning her world black. Her father,

whose thumbs were green, loved flowers. She dug

pockets for bulbs in reliable soil. Her petunias

shimmered pink and mauve, hemmed in

by flagstones along the driveway

where the red pickup was parked.

In the pickup's open bed

I stood, having grown to three and a half feet tall.

In her arms, my infant half-sister blotted

me out with her crying. I pointed, said, *She's horny*.

My mother's husband snickered

and looked me over. *Ornery,* he said

as my mother frowned.

*The word is ornery.*

# Labyrinth

She who bore me, supported my slack newborn neck
in her palm while she bathed me in a small basin,
warm water tested on her wrist

She who smoothed the auburn down of my brow, laundered
cotton diapers and stacked them four feet high
so she'd have enough

She who led me up and down stairs, whose hand meant home.
Who tickled freckles at bedtime as I sank,
sighing, into pillows.

She who ran cold vinegar baths for my sunburned skin.
Who covered me up in the sun, but shunned the darkness
I was in, in the garage

where her husband hussied me. Her voice made books
breathe while I held my tongue—*Don't tell*—
secret burning still,

long after her escape from him, leaving me as well.
*Abandonment,* it sounds so harsh, then and now,
well, doesn't it?

I still can't find her in the labyrinth of denial, and I envy
those who seem to live as though their mother never
existed, living or dead.

# Jogging Bra

        If breasts bounce in a figure 8 pattern on the body
of a woman

running, as described in a *New York Times*

            article about the history

      of the jogging bra, created by two jock straps
crossed

              it means penises must do the same

                  when men run.

      I used to practice figure 8s in ankle pinching skates

      My blades etched curved lines in ice, edged by
shirred trails of frozen lace

      I never saw my stepfather run. If he did, his penis danced in
a figure 8—

                  when he ran as a boy before I ran as
                  a girl.

Up across over down across back over up across and so on

      in an ellipse of motion.

              A wave if you will, turned

    sideways, never stops—like waves in a body of water

          pulled by the willful moon. Waves becoming waves.

                How willful our bodies in the act of obeying

        nature. I have stopped running from him and am always

      running.

                    People take a long time to die after they die.

Last night

      I saw my mother passing by

              ascending on the up escalator

as I descended. She smiled a cordial smile.

# Insomnia

When you left, mother,
at first I was numb.
Then feeling came back

as panic, little black feathers
folding softly over my mouth.
Still, sometimes, waking at 3 a.m.,

from star-darkness of sleep,
breathing lightly
in my creaturely self

questions wing
under ancient scar-stars:
Why did you go?

Why didn't I go with you?
My past stays alive
under your plumage.

# Ice Storm in Port Stanley

I remember frozen waves heaved onto sand
at the beach.

We had left the pickup truck nearby
and gone walking, kicking the rough edges
and spikes of ice.

We explored the spectacle of water stopped hard
by cold in its tumble to shore. It was like walking
around the brutal thought before its onslaught
from the tongue.

Instead of the conflict we were locked in
we were caught up, swept away
hands frozen, breath steaming
below a metallic sky, by something
the man called dad
and I were awed by.

# Giving Up on Revenge

Would you feel sorry for my husband, Ray,
just because he married me?
I'm the girl you resented having to raise.
At nights my sheets were territory
mapped by our battle over who had the right
to own me. You already possessed my mother.
Back then I was ten. And your goods. I lost that fight.
Who says the dead and living can't talk to each other?
Though you're beyond the grave and I'm still here
you're as close as the feeling of falling into
the thin place between forgiveness and fear.
Did anyone ever feel sorry for you?
I wish to surrender my right to avenge
for the sake of my children becoming men.

# Dwarf Beech in July

His blonde palomino Champ stood
sunlit in the paddock built by my stepfather,
who swore to make

animals cower like the grey mouse brought in by
our cat last night. Glimmering gelding
fourteen hands high didn't deserve his curses.

My grandparents admired my girlish penmanship then
in letters that left things out, the uncertain
comfort of the front room couch, the girl
staying put beneath her pink comforter.

He is dead now. So is the horse
and so is the mouse. On this rainy July day
in front of our house the dwarf beech
twirls its lime green umbrella
over its elaborately twisted trunk.

# Scar

Your smooth cheeks slapped
With Brut aftershave from the dark
Green bottle, onto your palms
Which gripped the wheel of the Ford
Pickup that drove us around fields
Tall with tobacco, wheat, corn or fallowed
With yellow ragweed, horsetail, bracken
Shepherd's purse, purslane, sorrel

Past gulches, gullies, ravines, ditches
Grown thick with milkweed and thistles
Shards of hidden brown glass, which
Once sliced a girl's ass which needed
Sutures to mend the wound which left
A ridge of tissue that never recovered

Feeling in its surface, soft as a peeled
Lychee beneath the fingertip trace
Of the grown woman's lovers

## Ombres Chinoises

Cutout figure

on a stick he

roams over her

childscape, hands

supplicating, he jaggeds across

stage to the princess

Pleads for black

bands to blot out

certain phrases

Fangs hang

chopping from

his top mandible

Her dress flares

a bell ringing above

skinny ankles

Ringlets chime

make her loud

Pang inside

pulls her to embrace

shoulders his

shaking as curtains close

# The Gaze

Her pony-tailed daughter,
I stand in the kitchen
pouring another glass of red wine.
She waits to be served
at my table now. Turning,
I catch my mother
looking at me, into me,
as if the lamp-lit moment itself
could reveal to her
who I am and where I've gone.
I pretend not to notice,
turn and rinse another glass.

Often, I drink in my boys'
four and six year-old faces
while they stare at the TV screen.
Since they're distracted
I can gorge
on their almond/chocolate/hazel eyes,
honey blonde and auburn heads.

I can't stop gazing at them
in the same way
she can't fold away
her longing.

II

# Taking Things Apart to Live

                      It was being in the once was
                      not knowing then
                      where now

In the long corridor
with linoleum floors
captains' light fixtures

          me carrying loads of laundry
          not being in the now

coming back to the apartment
children pulling at my life, legs

                      The one hiding in the crook
                      of my neck and shoulder
                      —the other volatile,

        taking things apart to live.

# Miscarriage

It is high summer. The day
is hot, harrowed, hallowed.

The doctor's words:
*nature is a terror.*

Gray needles grow
like stars clustered

on branches of the Blue Atlas Cedar
in the community garden.

Manhattan traffic roars alongside
a screen of laurel

vine debris rains
like green confetti.

# Sonogram

None of us carries the life we intended.
My body's core holds a stranger to me
unborn and unaware of a mother
alive with the howling of unmet needs
like pictures from unbearable dreams
from one generation to another
that demand to be uncovered and seen.

# Subway tunnel

Bronze patina of flame
resistant paint thickly rolled

and lavished on vaulted ceiling.
Trains rumble, crowds stumble

under Giotto's heaven
and Brooklyn.

I look up, like seeing
from the womb, rapt

before blinding delivery.

# The Braid

First, my cry, then yours, split the sky
above that Brooklyn hospital
as you, limbs curled and purple
slid out of my body
after a prolonged and irreversible journey.
Pain, then
absence of pain.

The midwife held you up,
newborn boy, alive in this world.
You peed an arc of urine
sparkling over the bed
and over her.

The champagne cork popped.
We all drank to life.
You suckled on a nipple.
Your lips still rimmed
with watery blood from that
other life inside.

We lay together, suspended,
holding on to each other.
Tough braid of blue and red
still binding us
cut for the first and last time.

# Newborn's Mouth

Breath the scent of apple slice
freshly cut sickle moon.

Tiny cavern of ridges and gums,
dark receiver of my aureole, nipple, milk.

His mouth suckling the first pleasure,
pulls the blue-white silk thread

from my body to his body
knitting us a blanket to curl up in

until his howl
and the next unraveling.

# Recognition

He'd been crying.
Now, I'm back.
His mouth, overflowing
with breast milk, drips over
my stomach, when he stops
sucking to look at me, relieved.
Shamelessly happy.

The way new lovers
stop kissing for a moment
just to look at each other
still shocked to have found
each other, and now
to be held, to behold!

The way I used to give myself
over and over to strangers.
It was always worth it
Even if I was used
even if I was rejected.

# Workday

Morning's the whine and clunk
of the elevator stopping on our floor.
My key turns, locks the door. As I run
for the bus I don't know

when I'll die
nor how dyslexia will affect
my son's life or which way
my marriage will go. While I'm at work

I remember the mineral smell
of my other son's scalp under
his nap of closely cropped hair.

In bed each evening I don't hear
sleep's wing beats as I drift
into houses not my own,
over continents, oceans

I don't hear the crack and roar
of melting polar ice, smell earth's
openings as it warms

can't feel the tides
rising and rising.

# Earn My Keep

Each week, we'd go out for fries and cheeseburgers,
my stomach a cave under my watering mouth.

Our wan waitress, twelve like me, carried our plates,
served us cokes, her mouth a line of string pulled straight.

My stepfather would say: *You see, she works to earn
her keep. We need to get you a job.*

That summer I snapped suckers from tobacco plants
taller than me. I worked in Ontario's sandy soil until

I had to stop, struck by mono. School started up
again in the fall and the decades stood and fell

and stamped him out. Now I'm looking for work
again to pay the bills, to buy my boys what they need

(and don't need). At home they lounge in front of screens,
sleep in when they can, do their chores,

work at being kind and doing well in school
and I'll keep on to earn their keep.

# Leap

This evening I linger in their room

longer than usual, resist my impulse to get out

away from them to peace and privacy.

Instead I yield to the buttery

nightlight shadows.

My hand scratches his lean, bare back.

When he says, "Mom, move your fingers

apart," there's a little leap in me,

glad he knows how to ask, as we lie there

precisely for what he wants.

# Rondeau After Meeting Her New Baby

You kept calling it Downer's Syndrome
in the dark car on the way home
after visiting a friend and her baby at the beach.
*Mom, his tongue sticks out even in his sleep.*
*Will he always do that? What's a chromosome?*

       *Before he was born, did his mother know?*
       Your school of questions ripple around
       my attempts to explain choice, biology.
       You kept calling it

what it wasn't yet the words you found
named an old sorrow in an odd song
we carried on our lips like salt from the sea,
tasted, swallowed, unseen.
Relentless as waves milling sand from stone
you kept calling.

# Clemency on the Q Train

A bee large as my thumb
turns in circles
on the black rubber floor
flecked with star speckled pattern
like outer space or a pebbled shore
under our feet
as the Q train rumbles home.

Silent subway riders
watch the bee lumber up
stumble across the blue
and white checkerboard
of a large tennis shoe

"Step on it!" someone says.
But I'll tell you quickly
he doesn't kill.

Awkwardly, gently, the shoe
nudges the bee
out into the clear space
between platform edge
and sliding door.

# Breadwinner

Key lime pie sits on fork's
tines in kitchen darkness. Plum
tomatoes glisten through
plastic cover.

I make the money,
you bring groceries home
in boxes each week,
towing food on a hand truck
putting cereal, bananas,
chicken and bread away.

One by one,
items get eaten or tossed,
then cupboards and fridge
empty again.

How I long to be alone.
To choose hunger.

# Layoff

Boss took the day off
the day I came back
to clean out my desk
that dead Friday in December.

I sit by the same window
same huge sky
stippled by clouds
like a wave pattern
from sandy beach vacations.
Is that the same hawk, circling?

I toss paper after dusty
paper. Sneeze. Release
pictures of my dear ones and me
from underneath bright
colored pins stuck
into the cloth wall.

Not much worth keeping.
What I take fits into a small box:
family photos, tea and shoes.
One pair pointed
and painful for meetings,
the other, rounded and flat
for walking away in.

# Motherhood Invents Me

Under house arrest and tired to my marrow

I bend down, again, to clean up their mess

My anger a tire iron

Two young sons, ruby-lipped, hair shining, want what I want

Food, play, and the sleep of dreams

To be told I'm good

But I can't go back to that life, before them

It brought me here

III

# Rafael's Question

My son carries the name
of the healing archangel. He

sits in my lap, at the computer's
luminous screen. We look at photos

of my parents, divorced
when I was two. Their faces

sagging, eyes hopeful.
Still alive, but their visits to us

number less than a handful
in his five year-old life.

Sometimes, after brushing our teeth
he'll say, "Mom, make it like a river."

And I'll cup my palms together
under running water, and he'll drink.

Tonight as we sit together
I'm silent, because it's hard to explain.

He asks me, "Do you still love them?"
So gently, so gently.

# Frontalier

You want your life back
can smell it like resin
of rotting leaves
despite the freezing wind

You want to live alone
in the timber-sided house
across the border in La Bâtie

You can walk from here
up the hilly wooded road
next to the thrashing river's
stone-stippled bed

Tall bare trees let light through
Arabian mare grazes at ravine's
edge above the mill

Table's set, wine's poured
motorway moans in your stomach
You can't stop the sound anymore
than you can grow jade quills
from your skin

The plumes in your mind
are pleats of stone
Winged Victory thunders
from the sky
a hymn swooping

hard against wind, drapery
plastered to powerful thighs
She can't ever land
because she has no eyes

# First night in Rougemont

"And the future holds the most remote event in union with what we most deeply want."
(Rainer Maria Rilke, from the *Sonnets to Orpheus*)


Standing in pine-scented wind
Mountain lit by full moon's opalescence
Church bells toll a full fifteen minutes

        Stained by October's alpine shadows
        I lift my full wine glass to the axis
        of church, moon and mountaintop

Inside, my children bask
in TV screen's hypnotic light
despite my calls to step into the chiming night

        When I open the door, they yell "no"
        pull the duvet to their chins
        a shield against the cold

You see, they want their story
and I want mine
though we live each other's

        So I stand alone
        watching mist from the valley rising
        like persistent and prodigal longing

# The Next Life

Could I come back as a tree?
A Blue Atlas Cedar
with star clusters for needles.
Wind, pale and blue,
sow my seeds in new
ground. Use bird beak,
insect and squirrel.
From here, that pine
leans like a torch song.
Sway, branch, sway.
Who wouldn't want that height,
those roots, that heft?
The silken spikes.

# Gill, Massachusetts

We must live here for now, in the
interstitial yet formative surprise
to the moment of next surprise when

the dog presents its friendly self. A boat
plows the lake, leaving a white rippled arrow
in its wake. Places of

the interstitial to enter into—
a place of thin time infused with summer:
cramped woods, an exodus of sounds

from feathered throats, reminders
of what keeps passing through something
like air.

# Large Subject; Small Poem

*Because it's infinite*

the boy dancer tells me

about his art,

each gesture

a wave

on the sea's

tinfoil surface

underneath

the magnet moon

# Hammurabi Replica at the International Labour Office

Stealing away from my fourth-floor desk,
drawn to the totem which stands
in the lobby, tall as a human body
rendered as an index finger. Alone

with it again, I place my hands
on its stone skin etched with cuneiform—
Babylonian laws, wages, punishments,

from knuckle to tip its words
ancient as the blood in my nail bed.

I hug its sun-warmed length. No one's
watching. Its stern tip could graze
a lip, hush a babe to sleep, brush
back hair from my face
pronounce my innocence.

# Blue Poles

What if we let
the self live
its transgressive life,
replaced matrimony
with polyamory in body
& mind & law?
What if we adhered
to Oscar Wilde's conviction:
pursuit of pleasure
as the highest ideal—
not ordeal?
Let the satyr seduce
the martyr within ourselves.
Let the lover's hand or our own
roam while the sermon revs.
Lived a happy, dangerous life—
like the blue poles in Jackson
Pollack's painting, standing tall,
held, yet leaning, ready to fall
in the magnificent swirl,
the chaos?

# Sky Eyes

If, after your plunge and breast stroke
you float on the surface
body embraced by wavelets,

inhabit your sky eyes.

In the flow and wash
of currents, overhear
pebbles click across
the stony bed.

Listen to their waterish warble

as the carbon in your blood
calls to their cold

mineral hearts—the tug
through a fathom's depth—
the span of distance between
your outstretched arms.

# Elegy for Leonard Cohen

Tonight the moon leans closer than it's been since 1948.
You were 14 then and tilted at longing. I wasn't born yet.

Hey, you missed the election of a fascist in the U.S.A.
You wouldn't be surprised. You'd write something for guitar,

of stars and bars, bloody and blue. Guess what
the president-elect says? He agrees with Howard

Stern—that women like me are best in bed because
they were abused as kids. They're wild

and hungry for love. Shame we never met,
but you were shoveling snow at your mountain hut

when I was still a crazy slut willing to be used for love.
Maybe we'll meet in another life—say, in half a million

years. Until then we'll call you up on the Ouija board
and look for you in the next super moon.

# Writing at the Convent of St. Helena

A wren
flits from screen
to screen in the pagoda,
trying to escape. Destiny
made me its rescuer.
I open the
door.

# Opened Up

Your need, that invisible
wound under scar—
finds him.

Hunger, shiver—
he puts his finger on it,
names it silver sliver

as though it could shine
its secret, a life apart,
as though it never knew

the jagged blade or you.

# Sanctuary

River road sways

Through an heirloom

Apple orchard

Below a forest

Silence sings

Spreads soft nets

For holding

Night's sorrow

A fire is lit

So red tongues

Can tell us things

We eat

We sleep

Under the world's wide roof:

Memory, shelter, escape

# The Bright Hem

The pupils
through which
the lovers view
the blue world
have become silt notes
trembling above the bed,
seeing what they cannot

below the window,
where a dozen tongues
swing in their metal cups,
ring through evening air—
follow the herder's
call, her French lilt
bending low, then tall,
over larkspur-meadowed alp.

This music old
and woven as days,
as white threads
sewn as Edelweiss
into leather bands
for cow bells.

In the bright hem of bliss
she sees the sweep
of him coming—from child
to man. He feels her blink
pound through the blood
of his whole body.

# Evensong

Six clangs, so it is 6:00 pm
according to the next village.

Birdsong still for the night.

Late November under this gray dome
between the Alps and Jura. We live

nearly all winter like this, ambling
through fog, chill, the comfort of

not seeing a mountain view. World
the color of mackerel. Sharp scent

of pine and lavender from the patch
of garden. I write with

frozen fingers, sitting on the bench

in front of our house. Planes
rumble at 8,000 feet. Here

on the ground I wonder how she,
meaning my mother, is getting along.

Campfire smell on this breezeless
night. She has asked me to stop writing

about her. I will go inside now to
warmth, to the bright orange

kitchen wall. If I had fur, I would
sleep outside all night in the cozy

dark, underneath the birdbath

next to the Chinese lantern plant,
berry faded inside its ragged paper

rib cage. In the morning,
I would be changed.

# All Born Perfect

Objects of my life
strewn across this table,
laid down in the precision of words:
green apples from a basket,
notebook and pen,
what I will say
and what I won't.

The old sorrow—
the one that won't go away
no matter how much
talking, pills, sex, wine,
even vengeance—
has become a blind dog now
its snout resting on paws.
Rilke said the dragons of fear
really just want our love.

The old sorrow remains
despite the distractions and good news
and good weather.
Even my children don't erase it.
Instead they gather
new ones for themselves
they imagine no one else carries,
all born perfect with howling needs.

Does anything change?
I have gone away to motherhood
and in that place where mothers stood
there is silence.

"You will write again," said Stanley Kunitz
in my dream.

"You will speak in a green voice
you hardly recognize."

# 5 a.m.

In the close noticing of things we become those things:
sky bright as wind chimes felt with closed eyes. Inside

the dream you wander shoeless
in supermarket aisles. Loneliness

opens its stone lid, invites you in. Even as they fly
birds trust in landings. In the right

tilt of rays you can become the silver thread
pinned to the eave,

the spider's wide swoop over
hayloft in honeyed light. Things

spiral inward and outward
at the same time—lines

drawn on your fingertips
before you were born

—the scrawl of maps survivors carry
to navigate belief, relief, grief: those streets lit

at dusk by a stream of thirst quenching
stars falling through the trees.

# I've Heard the Mermaids

In the night I go
swimming again

feathered
in dark

as the ship's
vermillion
sails are rent

as the seizure of
cargo begins;

I throw lifelines
to all the abused girls

at sea who
each make it
to shore alive

at first light
who sleep
who laugh

in a bed of
polyphonic song.

# About the Author

Carla Drysdale's first full-length collection of poems, *Little Venus,* was published in 2010 by Tightrope Books in Toronto. Her first chapbook of poems, *Inheritance,* came out with *Finishing Line Press* in 2016. Poems have appeared in numerous journals, including *Canadian Literature, Cleaver Magazine, Global City Review, LIT, Literary Mama, the Literary Review of Canada, PRISM international, The Fiddlehead,* and in the anthologies, *Entering the Real World: VCCA Poets on Mt. San Angelo* and *Nasty Women Poets.* In 2014 she was awarded the Earle Birney poetry prize for her poem, "Inheritance," by *PRISM international.* Born in London, Ontario, she lives with her husband and two sons in Ornex, France.

www.ingramcontent.com/pod-product-compliance
Lightning Source LLC
Chambersburg PA
CBHW021024090426

42738CB00007B/898